Coloring Book for Teens

Get Creative, Be Inspired, Have Fun, and Chill Out

CREATIVE COLORING PRESS

MILK
cute
CATS
PURR
I LOVE CA

Peace

WOOF
cute
DOGS
I LOVE

LOVE

I ♥ u

Summer
Summer
Summer
Summer

LOVE

hion
fashion
fashion
fas
fashion
fashion
fashion
fashi
fashion

Made in the USA
Monee, IL
06 December 2019

18004296R10046